#1 SONGS OF THE 90's

CLARINET

CONTENTS

This publication is not for sale in
the EC and/or Australia
or New Zealand.

ISBN 0-7935-3245-0

HAL•LEONARD™
CORPORATION

7777 W. BLUEMOUND RD. P.O. BOX 13819 MILWAUKEE, WI 53213

ACHY BREAKY HEART
(a.k.a. Don't Tell My Heart)

Words and Music by
DON VON TRESS

Clarinet

BABY BABY

Words and Music by AMY GRANT
and KEITH THOMAS

Clarinet

Moderately, not too fast

BLACK CAT

Words and Music by
JANET JACKSON

Clarinet

BLACK VELVET

Clarinet

Words and Music by CHRISTOPHER WARD
and DAVID TYSON

Moderately slow bluesey shuffle

BOOT SCOOTIN' BOOGIE

Words and Music by
RONNIE DUNN

Clarinet

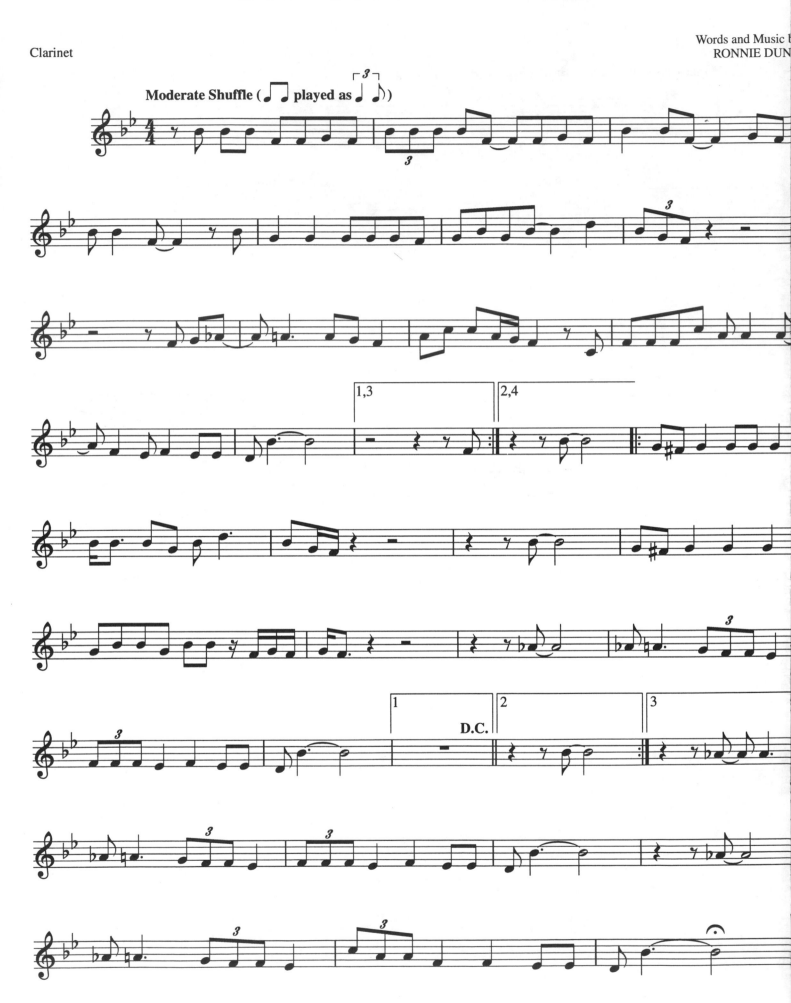

CAN'T HELP FALLING IN LOVE

Clarinet

Words and Music by GEORGE DAVID WEISS,
HUGO PERETTI and LUIGI CREATORE

DON'T LET THE SUN GO DOWN ON ME

Words and Music by ELTON JOHN
and BERNIE TAUPIN

Clarinet

DREAMLOVER

Clarinet

Words and Music by MARIAH CAREY
and DAVE HALL

EMOTIONS

Lyrics by MARIAH CAREY
Music by MARIAH CAREY,
DAVID COLE and ROBERT CLIVILLES

Clarinet

Moderate Dance tempo

GONNA MAKE YOU SWEAT
(Everybody Dance Now)

Clarinet

Words and Music by ROBERT CLIVILLE
and FREDERICK B. WILLIAM

Moderately Bright Rap

HOLD ON

Words by CARNIE WILSON
Words and Music by CHYNNA PHILLIPS
and GLEN BALLARD

Clarinet

MCA music publishing

HOW AM I SUPPOSED TO LIVE WITHOUT YOU

Clarinet

Words and Music by MICHAEL BOLTON
and DOUG JAMES

I DON'T HAVE THE HEART

Words and Music by ALLAN RICH
and JUD FRIEDMAN

Clarinet

MCA music publishing

I DON'T WANNA CRY

Words and Music by MARIAH CAREY
and NARADA MICHAEL WALDEN

Clarinet

I'D DO ANYTHING FOR LOVE
(But I Won't Do That)

Clarinet

Words and Music by
JIM STEINMAN

I'M YOUR BABY TONIGHT

Words and Music by BABYFACE
and L.A. REID

Clarinet

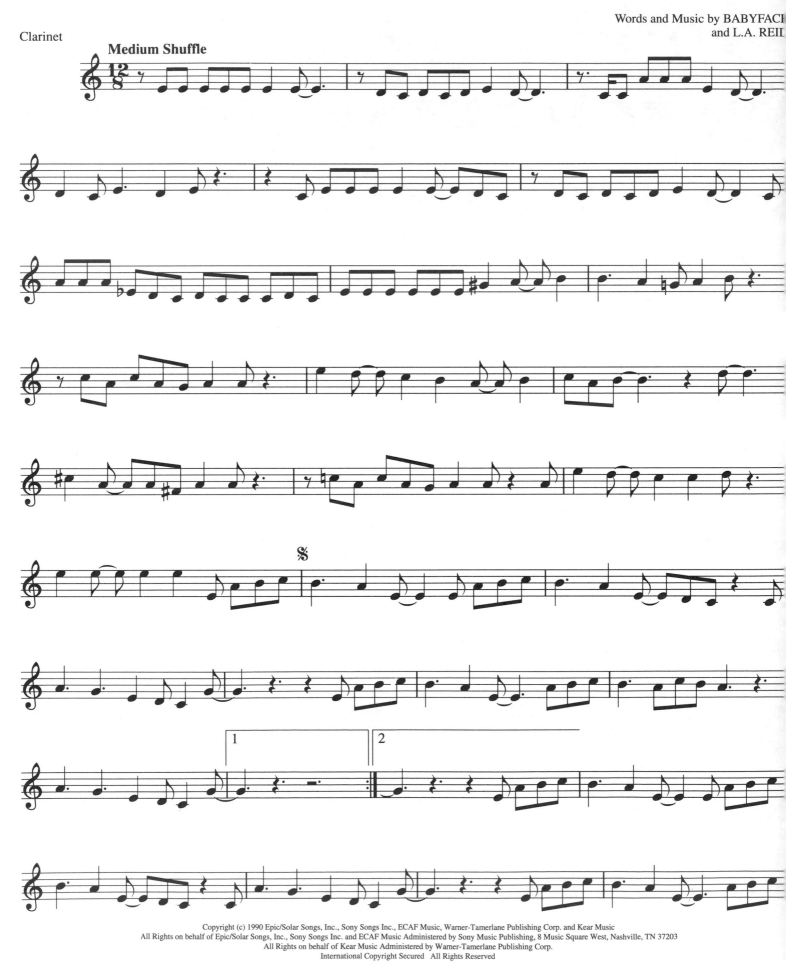

(Can't Live Without Your)
Love And Affection

Words and Music by MARC TANNER
MATT NELSON and GUNNAR NELSON

Clarinet

LOVE TAKES TIME

Words and Music by MARIAH CAREY
and BEN MARGULIES

PRAYING FOR TIME

Clarinet

Words and Music by
GEORGE MICHAEL

SAVE THE BEST FOR LAST

Words and Music by PHIL GALDSTON,
JON LIND and WENDY WALDMAN

SHAMELESS

Clarinet

Words and Music
BILLY JOEL

THIS USED TO BE MY PLAYGROUND
(From the Columbia Motion Picture "A LEAGUE OF THEIR OWN")

Words and Music by SHEP PETTIBONE
and MADONNA

Clarinet

MCA music publishing

TO BE WITH YOU

Words and Music by ERIC MARTIN
and DAVID GRAHAM

Clarinet